ON THE MOMMY TRACK is an original publication of Avon Books. This work has never before appeared in book form.

AVON BOOKS
A division of
The Hearst Corporation
105 Madison Avenue
New York, New York 10016

First Avon Books Trade Printing: May 1991

AVON TRADEMARK REG. U.S. PAT. OFF. AND IN OTHER COUNTRIES, MARCA REGISTRADA, HECHO EN U.S.A.

Printed in the U.S.A.

CW   10   9   8   7   6   5   4   3   2   1

CONTENTS

1

The Baby Album

Chapter Two
The Pregnancy

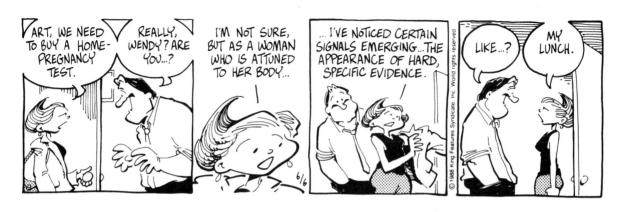

9

13

16

EVERY PREGNANCY IS DIFFERENT, BUT STILL, THE LADIES HERE HAVE A LOT IN COMMON!

IN FACT, RIGHT NOW YOU'RE ALL PROBABLY THINKING THE SAME THING...

"AT LEAST THE WOMAN NEXT TO ME HAS ANKLES MORE SWOLLEN THAN MINE."

IT'S PERFECTLY NATURAL FOR SOME WOMEN TO FEEL EMBARRASSED ABOUT BEING PREGNANT.

AT THESE CLASSES WE WANT TO MAKE YOU COMFORTABLE WITH YOURSELF. YOU'LL COME TO SEE THIS PROCESS AS THE HIGHEST ELEVATION OF HUMAN DIGNITY!

NOW LET'S ALL SIT ON THE FLOOR AND PANT LIKE DOGS.

22

The Baby Album

Chapter Three
The Birth

31

RIGHT NOW, ART, FOR THE FIRST TIME, I FEEL THAT WE'RE A FAMILY!

I'M GLAD WE'RE HAVING THIS MOMENT... THE THREE OF US, BONDING AS A SINGLE UNIT!

≡ SIGH ≡

OKAY, YOU CAN LET THE RELATIVES IN NOW.

3/18

A SET OF BLOCKS AND PLASTIC ANIMALS! THANKS, BOB! PATINA WILL LOVE THEM!

THREE NEWBORN JUMPSUITS! THANKS, GUYS!

A "LEARN TO READ" FLOPPY-DISK SYSTEM. THANKS, BUD!

3/20

A CALENDAR.

SEE? I'VE MARKED THE DATE YOUR MATERNITY LEAVE IS UP.

The Baby Album

Chapter Four
The Mommy Track

35

37

44

47

49

"FATHERHOOD USUALLY HAS A DEEP IMPACT ON MANY MEN.

"FREQUENTLY SOME EMBARK ON A FRENZIED SCRAMBLE TO MAKE MONEY, WORKING THEMSELVES RAGGED TO LIVE UP TO THE ROLE OF PROVIDER."

9/23

Billholbrook

DIT.

OKAY?

DON'T KNOCK YOURSELF OUT.

BELIEVE ME, BOB, PARENTHOOD CHANGES YOUR ENTIRE PERSPECTIVE ON THE WORLD!

YOU GAIN A WHOLE NEW SYSTEM OF VALUES... YOU DISCOVER NEW INSIGHT... YOU'RE CALLED TO A HIGHER PURPOSE IN LIFE!

10/31

BillHolbrook

IT'S...Y'KNOW, IT'S ALMOST LIKE A RELIGION!

EVER GET THE URGE TO SELL FLOWERS AT AIRPORTS?

ANYTHING TO GET OUT OF THE HOUSE ONCE IN A WHILE.

57

SAME THING HAPPENED TO ME, WENDY. AFTER HAVING A BABY, A WOMAN'S CO-WORKERS THINK LESS OF HER.

HOWEVER, WHEN A MAN BECOMES A FATHER, HIS ESTEEM INVARIABLY RISES!

REALLY? IS THAT ALWAYS TRUE?

2/3

WOW! LOOK AT ART HANDLE THE STRESSES OF PARENT-HOOD!

WHAT INNER FORTI-TUDE!

WE CAN ALL LEARN FROM THIS.

Z

SEE THAT THING ON THE WALL, PATINA? IT'S YOUR NURSERY INTERCOM!

IT LETS YOUR MOMMY HEAR YOU WHENEVER YOU'RE CRYING OR UPSET!

9/26

SAY HELLO TO MOMMY, PATINA!

GAA!

60

62

63

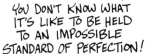

70

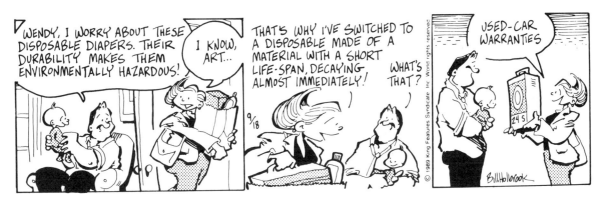

91

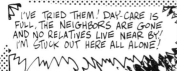

95

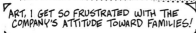
ART, I GET SO FRUSTRATED WITH THE COMPANY'S ATTITUDE TOWARD FAMILIES!

THEY'RE SO RIGID AND UNACCOMMODATING!

INSTEAD OF BEING FLEXIBLE, THEY WANT TOTAL CONTROL OVER US AT ALL TIMES!

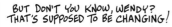
BUT DON'T YOU KNOW, WENDY? THAT'S SUPPOSED TO BE CHANGING!

I'D HEARD MS. TRELLIS IS TRYING TO CREATE MORE OF A "FAMILY ENVIRONMENT" AT WORK!

1/14

104

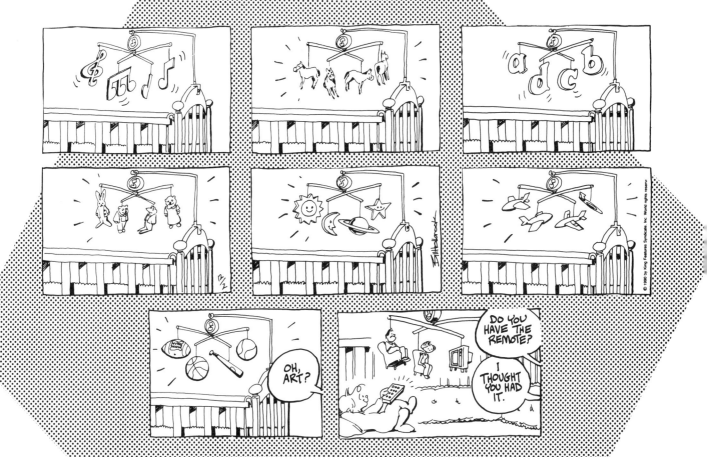

107

113